I Believe In You™

To your heart, your dream, and the difference you make.

Compiled by
Dan Zadra

Designed by
Kobi Yamada and Steve Potter

COM·PEN´·DI·UM™
Incorporated

Publishing and Communications

Acknowledgements

These quotations were gathered lovingly but unscientifically over several years and/or were contributed by many friends or acquaintances. Some arrived—and survived in our files—on scraps of paper and may therefore be imperfectly worded or attributed. To the authors, contributors and original sources, our thanks, and where appropriate, our apologies. —The Editors.

With Special Thanks To

John Applegate, Gerry Baird, Justi Baumgardt, Neil Beaton, Hal Belmont, Beth Bingham, Doug Cruickshank, Jim Darragh, Matthew Drummond, Josie and Rob Estes, Stephanie Floyd, Sarah Hunter, Holly Hughes, Jennifer Hurwitz, Scott Johnson, Dick Kamm, Beth Keane, Nick Krivokopich, Liam Lavery, Connie McMartin, Teri O'Brien, Janet Potter & Family, Diane Roger, Cristal Spurr, Robert & Val Yamada, Tote Yamada, Anne Zadra, Augie & Rosie Zadra and August & Arline Zadra.

Credits

Compiled by Dan Zadra

Designed by Kobi Yamada and Steve Potter

ISBN: 1-888387-29-7

Printed in Hong Kong

To your heart, your dream, and the difference you make.

Dedicated To You

Someone saw something in you once. That's partly why you are here today. Whoever it was had the wisdom and foresight to see your potential, to bet on your future, to catch hold of your dream.

In the game of life, maybe we should always be strong enough and sure enough to go it alone. Maybe it shouldn't matter whether someone else believes in us or not—but it does. There will always be lots of experts who can give us all the reasons why we shouldn't, we won't or we can't. That's why we cherish those rare individuals who are there to remind us why we should, why we will, why we can.

As the people in this little book remind us, it has always been so.

Two thousand years ago a 17 year old Egyptian girl wrote this message to her mother on a ragged piece of Papyrus that is still preserved in the Metropolitan Museum of Art: *Dear Mother, I'm all right. Stop worrying about me. Start believing in me.*

More than one hundred years ago Vincent van Gogh wrote this timeless message in his journal: "People must believe in each other, and feel that it can be done and must be done; in that way we are enormously strong. We must keep up each other's courage."

It was true then, and it's true now. All human progress has been the story of someone who believed passionately in something, and someone who believed passionately in that person. Whichever you are, this book is sincerely dedicated to you.

Here's to your heart, your dream, and the difference you make.

Dan Zadra

For Augie and Rosie

What do you pack to pursue a dream, and what do you leave behind?

—Sandra Sharpe

The first step in the journey
is to lose your way.

—Galway Kinnell

If we are going to do
anything significant with life,
we sometimes have to
move away from it—beyond
the usual measurements.
We must occasionally follow
visions and dreams.

—Bede Jarrett

Put your ear down
next to your soul
and listen hard.

—*Anne Sexton*

Life is too short and too
wonderful to waste time
doing things you really don't
want to be doing.

—*Bruce Isaacs*

Life is about turning
the things you really want to do
into the things you've done.

—*Smart Start*

8

What you already know is
merely a good departure point.

—Keorapetse Kgositsile

The dream is
not up there in the sky
or the stars, it's right
here in your heart.

—Dan Zadra

The future is sending back
good wishes, and waiting
with open arms.

—Kobi Yamada

Because of our routines
we forget that life is an
ongoing adventure.

—Maya Angelou

I had always wanted
an adventurous life. It took a
long time to realize that I was the
only one who was going to make an
adventurous life happen to me.

—Richard Bach

Your heart often knows things
before your mind does.

—Polly Adler

10

Make your own trail!

—Katharine Hepburn

An original life is
unexplored territory.
You don't get there
by taking a taxi—you get there
by carrying a canoe.

—Alan Alda

11

Go as far as you can see.
When you get there,
you can see farther.

—B.J. Marshal

Dreaming is a way
of travelling hopefully.

—Elizabeth David

Great hopes
make great lives.

—Dan Zadra

After all,
dreams are what
we live for.

—Tiffany Loren Rowe

Dreams are illustrations…
from the book your soul is
writing about you.

—*Marsha Norman*

Hope comes
furnished with light
and heat.

—*Don Ward*

13

Reach for your dreams
and they will reach for you.

—*Hana Rose Zadra*

We all have
many gifts that we've
never opened.   It's time to
open some of yours.
Find your wings!

—Dan Zadra

Everyone has inside him
a piece of good news.
The good news is that you
don't yet realize how great you
can be! How much you can love!
What you can accomplish!
And what your potential is!

—Anne Frank

Compared to the age of the
Universe, you are new to Nature.
No one can really predict to what
heights you might soar.
Even you will not know until
you spread your wings.

—Gil Atkinson

A boy found an eagle's egg and he put it in the nest of a prairie chicken. The eagle hatched and thought he was a chicken. He grew up doing what prairie chickens do—scratching at the dirt for food and flying short distances with a noisy fluttering of wings. It was a dreary life. Gradually the eagle grew old and bitter. One day he and his prairie chicken friend saw a beautiful bird soaring on the currents of air, high above the mountains.

I
Believe
In You.

"Oh, I wish I could fly like that!" said the eagle. The chicken replied, "Don't give it another thought. That's the mighty eagle, the king of all birds—you could never be like him!" And the eagle didn't give it another thought. He went on cackling and complaining about life. He died thinking he was a prairie chicken. My friend, you too were born an eagle. The Creator intended you to be an eagle, so don't listen to the prairie chickens!

—*Native American Legend*

Stretch your mind and fly.

—*African Proverb*

Reexamine all that you have
been told, or read in any books,
and dismiss whatever
insults your soul.

—*Walt Whitman*

There is more inside you
than you dare think.

—*David Brower*

We all have
the extraordinary coded within us,
waiting to be released.

—*J. L. Houston*

We know what we are,
but know not what we may be.

—*William Shakespeare*

19

The exciting qualities you
see in others also exist in you.
You may not be able to see your
potential, but it's there,
and it is enormous!

—*EDGE Keynote*

When you were born,
God said, 'Yes!'

—Unknown

You're not here by mistake.

—Ben Morrow

I believe everyone is born into
the world to do something unique
and something distinctive.

—Benjamin E. Mays

Each of us is uniquely different.
Like snowflakes, the human pattern
is never cast twice.

—*Alice Childress*

You are an unrepeatable miracle.

—*Diane Roger*

21

There are billions of people
in the world, and every one of
them is special. No one else in
the world is like you.

—*Muhammad Ali*

Nature never made
a nobody. Everybody was
born with some kind of talent.

—*Melvin Chapman*

Everyone has a unique role
to fill in the world. Everyone,
including and perhaps especially
you, is indispensable.

—*Nathaniel Hawthorne*

There are many wonderful
things that will never be done
if you do not do them.

—*Charles D. Gill*

22

Talents, small or large,
are God-given. They are
a sacred trust.

—*Paul Robeson*

One of the marks of a gift
is to have the courage to fulfill it.

—*Katherine Ann Porter*

What you do matters.
All you need is to do it.

—*Judy Grahn*

23

A No. 2 pencil
and a dream can
take you
anywhere.

—Joyce A. Myers

What if the Hokey-Pokey
really is what it's all about?

—Unknown

You see, there is no more
purpose or meaning in the world
than you put into it.

—Hans Reichenbach

A great goal in life is the
only fortune worth finding.

—Jacqueline Kennedy Onassis

An elderly man, in the final days
of his life, is lying in bed alone.
He awakens to see a large group
of people clustered around his bed.
Their faces are loving, but sad.
Confused, the old man smiles
weakly and whispers, 'You must
be my childhood friends, come to
say good-bye. I am so grateful.'
Moving closer, the tallest figure
gently grasps the old man's hand
and replies, 'Yes, we are your best

I
Believe
In You.

and oldest friends, but long ago
you abandoned us. For we are the
unfulfilled promises of your youth.
We are the unrealized hopes, dreams
and plans that you once felt deeply
in your heart, but never pursued.
We are the unique talents that you
never refined, the special gifts you
never discovered. Old friend, we
have not come to comfort you,
but to die with you.'

—Les Brown

27

I dare you, while
there is still time, to have a
magnificent obsession.

—William Danforth

How do you
want to be remembered?

—Kobi Yamada

What great thing would you
attempt if you knew
you could not fail?

—Dr. Robert H. Schuller

Set your goals to paper
and you're halfway there!

—*Don Ward*

Close your eyes and imagine
that you are being interviewed
on your 100th birthday. What are
the five top things you would love
to be able to tell the reporters that
you have accomplished? Now open
your eyes and write them down.
You have a fresh start on life!

—*EDGE Keynote*

29

Your willingness to
create a new dream or
vision for your life is a statement
of belief in your own potential.

—*David McNally*

It's seizing the day
and accepting responsibility
for your future. It's seeing what
other people don't see, and
pursuing that vision no matter
who tells you not to.

—*Howard Schultz, Starbucks*

The reason most people never reach their goals is that they don't seriously consider them as believable or achievable.

—Denis Waitley

Your hopes, dreams and aspirations are legitimate.
They are trying to take you airborne, above the clouds, above the storms— if you will only let them!

—Diane Roger

That is happiness;
to be dissolved into something complete and great.

—Willa Cather

Let me
listen to me
and not
to them.

—Gertrude Stein

Form the habit of
saying 'Yes' to your good ideas.
Then write down all the reasons
why they will work. There will always
be plenty of people around to
tell you why they won't work.

—*Gil Atkinson*

33

They'll tell you, 'Quit now,
you'll never make it.'
If you disregard that advice,
you'll be halfway there.

—*David Zucker*

As a dreamer, you will be
laughed at...Thank them!

—Unknown

Virtually all new ideas
which have resulted in change
in our society were at one time
scorned or illegal. All progress
involves flying in the face of
old rules that no longer apply.
People ridiculed the Edisons,
Einsteins and Madame Curies—
until they were successful.

—EDGE Keynote

Even when the experts all agree,
they may well be mistaken.

—Bertrand Russell

For 1,500 years, the Earth
was the center of the Solar System
simply because Claudius Ptolemy
said so. A week before Kittyhawk,
a New York science editor proved
that heavier-than-air-flight was
impossible. Experts at first said
James Joyce couldn't write, Picasso
couldn't paint, and Elvis couldn't sing.
What do they say about you?

—Dare To Be Different

I
Believe
In You.

What great achievement
has been performed by the one
who told you it couldn't be done?

—Melvin Chapman

People will try to tell you that
all the great opportunities
have been snapped up. In reality,
the world changes every second,
blowing new opportunities in all
directions, including yours.

—Ken Hakuta

Most people see what is,
and never see what can be.

—*Albert Einstein*

If people don't agree
with you, so what? If people agree
with you, so what?

—*Dr. Robert Anthony*

Set your course by the stars, not by
the lights of every passing ship.

—*Gen. Omar Bradley*

Once in awhile it really hits
people that they don't have to
experience the world in the way
they have been told to.

—*Alan Keightley*

Don't let other people
tell you who you are.

—*Diane Sawyer*

There is only one you.
God wanted you to be you.
Don't you dare change just
because you're outnumbered!

—*Charles Swindoll*

Talk back to your internal critic.

—Robert McKain

Try very hard not to lose
your dream or your ideal. It is
not easy to find it once you
have lost it—the pressure of
life is too strong by then.

—Frank Lloyd Wright

39

Try very hard not to lose your dream or your ideal.

The greatest gift you will
ever receive is the gift of loving
and believing in yourself. Guard this
gift with your life. It is the only thing
that will ever truly be yours.

—Tiffany Loren Rowe

I
Believe
InYou™

To go against the dominant
thinking of your friends, of most
of the people you see every day,
is perhaps the most difficult act
of heroism you can have.

—*Theodore White*

Hell would be if God were
to show me things I could
have accomplished if only
I had believed in myself.

—*Unknown*

Think for yourself.
No one else is qualified.

—Frank Vizarre

Listen to the mustn'ts, child,
listen to the don'ts—listen to
the shouldn'ts, the impossibles,
the won'ts—listen to the never
haves, then listen close to me—
anything can happen, child.
ANYTHING can be.

—Shel Silverstein

You must
take your chance.

—William Shakespeare

Up, you mighty people,
you can accomplish
what you will!

—*Marcus Garvey*

Ain't no chance
if you don't take it.

—*Guy Clark*

Do whatever your
heart leads you to do—
but do it.

—*Truman X. Jones*

Every day you sit back
and wait for something to
happen is another day lost.

—*Jennifer Flavin*

44

We cannot put off living until
we are ready. The most salient
characteristic of life is its urgency,
'here and now' without any
possible postponement.
Life is fired at us point-blank.

—*Jose Ortega y Gasset*

I
Believe
InYou.

Faith is daring to put your
dream to the test. It is better
to try to do something and fail
than to try to do nothing
and succeed.

—Dr. Robert H. Schuller

There is the risk
you cannot afford to take,
and there is the risk you
cannot afford not to take.

—Peter Drucker

When the defining moment comes,
either you define the moment,
or the moment defines you.

—Tin Cup

To every person there comes
that moment when he is figuratively
tapped on the shoulder to do a
very special thing unique to him.
What a tragedy if that moment
finds him unprepared for the work
that would be his finest hour.

—Winston Churchill

After you have made
up your mind just what
you are going to do, is a
good time to do it.

—Josh Billings

Are you in earnest?
Then seize this very minute.
Whatever you can do, or dream you
can, begin it. Boldness has genius,
power and magic in it. Only engage
and then the mind grows heated;
only begin, and then the
goal will be completed.

—Goethe

There are some decisions in life
that only you can make.

—Merle Shain

No trumpets sound
when the important decisions
of our lives are made.

—Agnes De Mille

The real moment of success
is not the moment apparent
to the crowd.

—George Bernard Shaw

I
Believe
InYou.

I always believed that if
you set out to be successful,
then you already are.

—Katherine Dunham

The aim, if reached or not,
makes great the life.

—Robert Browning

Determine that the thing
shall be done, and then we
shall find the way.

—Abraham Lincoln

When you
think at that moment
that it is possible—
then the magic starts.

—Siegfried

The longest journey
you will ever take is the
18 inches from your head
to your heart.

—Andrew Bennett

Once you
accept an idea, it's an idea
whose time has come.

—William James

High intention sets the
universe in motion.

—Armand Hammer

Be assured that any
worthwhile action will create
change and attract support.

—Philip Marvin

If you believe in yourself,
so will others.

—Graham Greene

We all wish you happiness
and we will support you, help you,
cheer for you. But our wishes
cannot give you success.
It can only come from yourself,
from the spirit within you.

—Rev. W. Ralph Ward, Jr.

I realized a long time ago
that a belief which does not
spring from a conviction in the
emotions is no belief at all.

—*Evelyn Scott*

You must find the passion,
an unrelenting passion.

—*David Easton*

53

For it's not light that is needed, but fire;
it's not the gentle shower, but thunder.
We need the storm, the whirlwind and
the earthquake in our hearts.

—*Frederick Douglass, 1852*

Something we were
withholding made us weak,
until we found it was ourselves.

—Robert Frost

When you hold back on life,
life holds back on you.

—Mary Manin Morrissey

What convinces is conviction.

—Lyndon Baines Johnson

The one piece of advice which
will contribute to making you a better
leader, will provide you with greater
happiness and will advance your
career more than any other advice…
and it doesn't call for a special
personality or any certain chemistry…
and any one of you can do it.
And that advice is: You must care.

—Lt. General Melvin Zais

Bad things don't happen
because you care, they happen
when you don't care.

—Elizabeth Matthews

Women are repeatedly
accused of taking things personally.
I cannot see any other honest
way of taking them.

—*Marya Mannes*

We're not sent into this world
to do anything into which we
cannot put our hearts.

—*John Ruskin*

If you want to make
the days in your life really matter,
then you must love something.

—*Kobi Yamada*

The five happiest people
I have ever met all had this
strange little quirk of referring
to their jobs as a 'calling.'

—Eric Sevareid

There is forward motion to yearning.

—Gail Godwin

If you are working on something
exciting that you really care about,
you don't have to be pushed.
The vision pulls you.

—Steve Jobs

If it doesn't absorb you,
if you don't love it, don't do it.

—D.H. Lawrence

★

I don't think you should
ever manage something that
you don't care passionately about.

—Deborah Coleman

★

I personally don't know how
anybody can survive running a
successful business in our times
without caring. The twin ideals of love
and care touch everything we do.

—Anita Roddick

I
Believe
In You.

Anything will
give up its secrets if
you love it enough.

—George Washington Carver

If the love of what you're doing
exceeds the labor of doing it...
success is inevitable.

—Bob Beers

And will you succeed?
Yes indeed, yes indeed.
Ninety eight and three-quarters
percent guaranteed!

—Dr. Seuss

59

Do not fear mistakes.
There are none.

—Miles Davis

Mistakes are a fact of life.
It is the response to error
that counts.

—Nikki Giovanni

I have missed more than 9,000
shots in my career. I have lost almost
300 games. On 26 occasions I have
been entrusted to take the game–
winning shot…and missed. I have
failed over and over again in my life.
And that is why I succeed.

—Michael Jordan

61

You failed many times,
although you may not remember.
You fell down the first time you
tried to walk. You almost drowned
the first time you tried to swim,
didn't you? Did you hit the ball the
first time you swung a bat?
Babe Ruth struck out 1,330 times,
but he also hit 714 home runs.
Don't worry about failure.
Worry about the chances you
miss when you don't try.

—*United Technologies*

You've got to have a safe
environment where people can
make mistakes and learn from them.
If we're not making mistakes,
we're not going anywhere.

—Gordon Forward

When starting a new project,
try to make as many mistakes
as rapidly as possible in order to
learn as much as you can in the
shortest period of time.

—Bob Moawad

If you make a mistake,
acknowledge it quickly
and openly, learn from it,
forget it and move on.

—Brian Tracy

Rather than admit a mistake,
nations have gone to war,
families have separated, and
good people have sacrificed
everything dear to them.
Admitting that you were wrong is
just another way of saying that you
are wiser today than yesterday.

—Don Ward

Those who aren't
making mistakes probably
aren't making anything.

—*Samuel Smiles*

Trial and error is the secret sauce
of the creative process. By finding out
what doesn't work, we eventually
discover what does.

—*Mistakes Are Great*

65

Fail? I haven't failed! I now know
3,800 ways not to make an
electric storage battery.

—*Thomas Edison*

Treat failure as practice shots.

—Deborah McGriff

Wrong turns are as
important as right turns.
More important sometimes.

—Richard Bach

Sometimes you have to lose
major championships before you
can win them. Losing is a learning
experience that's worth a fortune.

—Tom Watson

Never mistake a clear
view for a short distance.

—*Mark Spain*

There are no shortcuts
to any place worth going.

—*Beverly Sills*

All have disappointments,
all have times when
it isn't worthwhile.

—*John H. Johnson*

Celebrate those
who attempt great things,
even though they fail.

—*Seneca*

Look the world straight in the eye.

—*Helen Keller*

I didn't lose the gold.
I won the silver.

—*Michelle Kwan*

Failing doesn't make you a failure. Failure is an occurrence rather than a person.

—Dick Anderson

Just aim to do your best and mankind will give you credit where you fail.

—Thomas Jefferson

69

The only failure is to grow old and not to have tried.

—Beatrice Colen

I Believe In You™

Be special,
be anything but
mediocre.

—Anita Roddick.

Come give us
a taste of your quality.

—*William Shakespeare*

Be so good
they can't ignore you.

—*Jerry Dunn*

This is your life,
your one and only life—
so take excellence
very personally.

—*Scott Johnson*

I
Believe
In You™

No calling on earth is
insignificant if it is accomplished
with pride and artistry.

—Gil Atkinson

The French fry is my canvas.

—Ray Kroc

No matter what your
role is in the business of life,
the goal is quality and the
challenge is reaching it.

—Fred Smith, Founder of Federal Express

Whoever I am or
whatever I am doing,
some kind of excellence
is within my reach.

—John Gardner

If a man is called to be a
streetsweeper, he should sweep
streets even as Michelangelo painted
or Beethoven composed music or
Shakespeare wrote poetry. He should
sweep streets so well that all the
hosts of heaven and earth will
pause to say, 'Here lived a great
streetsweeper who did his job well.'

—Martin Luther King, Jr.

A company's character
is known by the people
it keeps.

—John Ruskin

Being a good human being
is good business.

—Paul Hawken

Live and work with
integrity, and everything else
is a piece of cake.

—Pat Salvatore

The best companies assume
that each individual wants to make
a difference in the world and be
respected. Is that a surprise?

—Paul Ames

We are not here merely
to make a living. We are
here to enrich the world with
a finer spirit of hope and
achievement—and we
impoverish ourselves if
we forget the errand.

—Woodrow Wilson

75

Believe that
there's light at the
end of the tunnel.
Believe that you
may be that light
for someone else.

—Kobi Yamada

I was successful
because you believed in me.

—A Friend

No one can go it alone.
Somewhere along the line is
the person who gives you faith
that you can make it.

—Grace Gil Olivarez

I have flown because
you gave me wings.

—Wedding Verse

Surround yourself with people
who believe you can.

—*Dan Zadra*

If someone believes in you,
and you believe in your dreams,
it can happen.

—*Tiffany Loren Rowe*

You can work miracles
by having faith in others.
To inspire the best in people,
choose to think and believe
the best about them.

—*Bob Moawad*

We relish news of our heroes,
forgetting that we are special
to someone, too.

—Marva Collins

All of you reading these words
have loved someone, have done
someone a kindness, have healed a
wound, have taken on a challenge,
have created something beautiful,
and have enjoyed breathing the air
of existence. Every moment
you make a difference.

—Random Acts of Kindness

Friends are kind
to each other's hopes.
They cherish each other's dreams.

—Henry David Thoreau

★

There are low spots in our lives,
but there are also high spots, and
most of them have come through
encouragement from someone else.

—George M. Adams

★

If I made it, it's half because
I was game enough to take a lot of
punishment along the way and half
because there were a lot of people
who cared enough to help me.

—Althea Gibson

If someone listens, or stretches
out a hand, or whispers a kind
word of encouragement, or attempts
to understand, extraordinary
things begin to happen.

—*Loretta Girzartis*

How did I get here? Somebody
pushed me. Somebody must have
set me off in this direction and
clusters of other hands must have
touched themselves to the controls
at various times, for I would not have
picked this way for the world.

—*Joseph Heller*

If you don't look out for others,
who will look out for you?

—Whoopi Goldberg

You get nervous with no one
supporting you. People don't always
have the vision, and the secret for the
person with the vision is to stand up.
But it takes courage. You get lonely.

—Natalie Cole

To love a person is to learn the song
that is in their heart, and to sing it to
them when they have forgotten.

—Thomas Chandler

Treasure the one who is
thinking of you when all others
are thinking of themselves.

—*James Gunn*

If you're scared,
just holler and you'll find it ain't
so lonesome out there.

—*Joe Sugdenpage*

We are, none of us,
all alone in the world.
Your brothers are here, too.

—*Dr. Albert Schweitzer*

We must convey to children
that we believe in them.

—Marian Wright Edelman

Do I believe I'm blessed?
Of course I do! In the first place,
my mother told me so many, many
times, and when she did it was always
quietly, confidently…and I knew that
anything she told me was true.

—Duke Ellington

My father's quiet example lit
up my life and our town.

—Carol O'Leary

There are wide-eyed
little people who believe you're
always right; and their eyes are
always opened, and they watch
you day and night. You're the little
people's idol, you're the wisest
of the wise. In their little minds
about you no suspicions ever rise.
You are setting an example
every day in all you do, for the
little ones who are waiting to
grow up to be like you.

—Unknown

All we can ask
in our lives is that perhaps
we can make a little difference
in someone else's.

—Lillian Davis, founder, Ivymount School

★

Each of us can look back
upon someone who made
a great difference in our lives,
often a teacher whose wisdom
or simple acts of caring made
an impression upon us at a
formative time. In all likelihood,
it was someone who sought no
recognition for their deed, other than
the joy of knowing that, by their hand,
another's life had been made better.

—Stephen M. Wolf

If someone can stand on
my shoulders and take their
dream to a higher level,
maybe that's success, too.

—*Steve Potter*

One can do anything,
anything at all, if provided with a
passionate and gifted teacher.

—*Pat Conroy*

He was the father, brother,
friend I never had. He told me he was
proud of me. No one else ever said that.

—*A Student's eulogy for Jonathan Leven,
high school English teacher.*

You really
can change
the world
if you
care enough.

—Marion Wright Edelman

We are the ones
we've been waiting for.

—June Gordon

★

We grow up thinking that
the best answer is in someone
else's brain.   Much of our education
is an elaborate game of 'guess what's
in the teacher's head?' What the
world really needs to know
right now is what kind of dreams
and ideas are in your head.

—Roger von Oech

I
**Believe
In**You.

We have it in our power
to begin the world again.

—Thomas Paine, 1776

We made the world we're living in
and we can make it over.

—James Baldwin

Once and for all, let's harness the
extraordinary dreams of our young
people to the experience and
know-how of their parents.

—John F. Kennedy

Never tell a young person
that something can't be done.
God may have waited centuries
for someone ignorant enough of
the impossible to do that very thing.

—Michael LeBoeuf

You don't have to be tall
to see the moon.

—African Proverb

I am tired of hearing that
our country doesn't work—
it isn't supposed to work.
We are supposed to work it.

—Alexander Woolcott

Leadership is action,
not position.

—D.H. McGannon

The times do not allow anyone
the luxury of waiting around for
others to lead. All can lead and
ought to be invited to do so.

—Matthew Fox

Your spark can become
a flame and change everything.

—E.D. Nixon

Everyone has an opportunity
to be great because everyone has
an opportunity to serve.

—Martin Luther King, Jr.

We are here to add
what we can to, not to get what
we can from, life.

—Sir William Osler

Love in action is the force
that will set us free.

—Susan Taylor

93

Have faith in yourself.
But have faith in your friends and neighbors, too. I know life is competitive—but it isn't a jungle. Like begets like. Faith inspires faith. People give back substantially what we give them.

—*Bethany College Commencement Address*

Most people are like you and me, or the people across the street or around the world from you and me. Just like you and me, their hearts tell them that somewhere, somehow they can make a positive difference in the world.

—*William Baker*

Realize how good
you really are.

—*Og Mandino*

Find the good.
It's all around you.
Find it, show it to others,
and you'll start believing in it.

—*Jesse Owens*

Assume that people
are good until you actually
and specifically learn differently.
And even then, know that they
have potential for change and
that you can help them out.

—*Leo Buscaglia*

I
Believe
In You™

We can't move ahead
if we're trying to get even.

—Frank Tyger

We can't solve problems
by drifting backwards;
we solve them by tearing
down barriers so we
can get at them.

—Benjamin Mays

The most powerful
agent of change is
a change of heart.

—B.J. Marshal

Courage calls
to courage everywhere.

—Millicent Fawcett

We have to find ways
of organizing ourselves with
the rest of humanity. It has to be
everybody or nobody.

—Buckminster Fuller

The whole is
the sum of the parts.
Be a good part.

—Nate McConnell

If you're too busy
to help those around you,
you're too busy.

—Bob Moawad

If I am not for myself, who will be for me?
If I am not for others, who am I for?
And if not now, when?

—Talmud

Let no one come to you
without leaving better.

—Mother Teresa

The whole idea of living
is to believe the best is yet to be.

—*Peter Ustinov*

If we want to make something
really superb of our community
and this planet, there is nothing
whatever can stop us.

—*Shepherd Mead*

Together, we have the power,
knowledge and equipment to
build a world beyond our wonder.
Only loss of nerve can defeat us.
That is all—loss of nerve.

—*James Dillet Freeman*

I
Believe
In You.

If you're going
through hell,
keep going.

—Rob Estes

What courage it takes
to believe in a dream.

—Carlos Menta

What saves a person is to
take a step, then another step.

—Antoine De Exupery

You got yourself this far—
you just got to keep going.

—Don Ward

In the face of uncertainty,
there is nothing wrong with hope.

—Bernie Siegel

In times of difficulty, you may feel
that your problems will go on and on,
but they won't. Every mountain has
a top. Every problem has a life span.
The question is, who is going to
give in first, the frustration or you?

—Dr. Robert H. Schuller

Don't ever lose hope.
It works.

—Jewel

I
Believe
In You.

Life is not the way it's
supposed to be. It's the way it is.
The way you deal with it is what
makes the difference.

—Virginia Satir

You are never powerless.

—Jane Seymour

We cannot tell what may happen
to us in the strange medley of life.
But we can decide what happens in us,
how we take it, what we do with it—and
that is what really counts in the end.

—Joseph Fort Newton

Out of every crisis comes
the chance to be reborn.

—Nena O'Neill

Courage is believing in yourself
in the worst moments, and that's
something nobody can teach you.
I have never heard of a University
of Bravery, but I do know that
everyone has it in them to be brave.

—El Cordobes

The best thing in life
should be courage.

—Robert Frost

Most people don't know
how brave they really are.

—R.E. Chambers

A hero is simply someone
who rises above his or her own
human weaknesses, for an
hour, a day, a year, to do
something stirring.

—Betty Deramus

Our fears must never hold us back
from pursuing our hopes.

—John F. Kennedy, Profiles In Courage

I
Believe
In You™

Every now and then,
bite off more than you can chew.

—Kobi Yamada

Forget your excuses.
Records are set all the time by
big-hearted people who didn't
have the right background,
experience or ability—or who
just didn't know any better.

—To Your Success

I was dirt poor, blind, you name it.
Yet here I am today.

—Ray Charles

106

We are not creatures of circumstance;
we are creators of circumstance.

—*Benjamin Disraeli*

Too young or too old is no excuse.
Wrong color is no excuse. In debt
is no excuse. There's simply no
bona fide, genuine excuse for
not being super-successful.
You control what you become.

—*Scott Alexander*

A bad attitude is the only
true handicap.

—*Scott Hamilton*

I
Believe
In You.

I think I can break the odds.

—*Jose Fernandez*

There is no such thing
as no chance.

—*Henry Ford*

No matter what the statistics say,
there's always a way.

—*Bernie Siegal*

The bible says,
'All things are possible.'
I believe that.

—Dolly Parton

Never give up.
This may be your moment
for a miracle.

—Greg Anderson

If you're going
to doubt something,
doubt your limits.

—Don Ward

I
Believe
In You.

I took an inventory and looked
into my little bag to see what I had
left over. I had one jewel left in
the bag, the brightest jewel of all.
I had the gift of faith.

—Lola Falana

It gets dark sometimes, but
morning comes…Keep hope alive.

—Jesse Jackson

Believing in yourself is an
endless destination. Believing
you have failed is the end
of your journey.

—Sarah Meredith

I
Believe
InYou.

Hang in there. Many of life's failures are people who did not realize how close they were to success when they gave up.

—Thomas Edison

He who has a 'why' to live for can bear with almost any 'how.'

—F. Nietzsche

Instead of 'we almost,' let the world say about us, 'we did.'

—Don Ward

It's what you do,
not when you do it,
that counts.

—Dan Zadra

You lose a lot of speed between
80 and 86.

—Ruth Rothfarb, 86
(On not improving her personal best in the marathon)

On his 103rd birthday,
Cal Evans was interviewed by a
Denver reporter. 'Have you lived
in Denver all your life?' asked
the reporter. 'Not yet, sonny,'
Cal replied.

—Keep On Keepin' On

★

I'm not going to die, I'm going home
like a shooting star.

—Sojourner Truth

113

Still I am learning.

—Michelangelo

Don't tell people how old you are—
tell them about your goals and what
you are doing to attain them.

—Guy Clarke

Dreams are renewable.
Whether you're five or 105,
you have a lifetime ahead of you.

—Rev. Dale Turner

At age 7, Mozart wrote his
first symphony. At 12, Shane Gould
won an Olympic medal. At 14,
Leann Rimes topped the Country
music charts. At 17, Joan of Arc
led an Army in defense of Europe.
At 57, Ray Kroc founded McDonald's.
At 71, Michelangelo painted the
Sistine Chapel. At 80, George
Burns won his first Oscar. At 104,
Cal Evans wrote his first book
on the American West.

—*Gil Atkinson*

People who never get carried away,
should be.

—Malcolm Forbes

Every ten years
we should all give ourselves
a good kick in the pants.

—Edward Steichen

If you have a friend or co-worker
who hasn't discarded a major opinion
or acquired a new one in several years,
check their pulse. They may be dead.

—Gelett Burgess

There is nothing
more beautiful in life than
getting a second chance.

—Ron Kovic

It's never too late,
in fiction or in life, to revise.

—Nancy Thayer

I'd rather be sorry
for something I did than
for something I didn't do.

—Red Scott

Normal day, let me be aware
of the treasure you are.

—*Mary Jean Irion*

If children with terminal
cancer can find love, joy,
meaning and purpose in each day—
and they do—why can't we?

—*Dan Zadra*

If you had five minutes to live,
who would you call and
why are you waiting?

—*Michael Nolan*

Each morning he'd stack up
the letters he'd write—tomorrow.
And think of the friends
he'd fill with delight—tomorrow.
It was too bad, indeed,
he was busy today,
And hadn't a minute
to stop on his way.
'More time I'll give to others,'
he'd say,—tomorrow.
But the fact is he died and
faded from view, and all that he left
when the living was through,
Was a mountain of things he
intended to do—tomorrow.

—Unknown

We believe that life is measured in memories, not years.

—Make-A-Wish Foundation

You may not recognize success
when it happens. It's not always
the thing you expected it to be.
Looking back, you will realize that
there are successes to be recognized
and joy to be seized in every day.

—*Elizabeth Keane*

My life now, my whole life apart
from anything that can happen to me,
every minute of it has the positive
meaning of goodness which I still
have the power to put into it.

—*Konstantine Levin, Anna Karenina*

If I never met you, I would have dreamed you into being.

—Sebastian Chantoix

★

There are many compliments that may come to an individual in the course of a lifetime, but there is no higher tribute than to be loved by those who know us best.

—Dr. Dale E. Turner

★

Life and love are all we get, so life and love are all we can give.

—Dan Zadra

Everyone has a gift for
something, even if it is the gift
of being a good friend.

—Marian Anderson

I only wish you could see
what I see when I look at you.

—Kobi Yamada

123

By being yourself, you put
something wonderful in the world
that was not there before.

—Edwin Elliot

I
Believe
In You™

At the end of life,
our questions are very simple.
Did I live fully? Did I love well?

—Jack Kornfield

On Judgement Day
if God should say, 'Did you clean
your house today?' I will say,
'I did not. I played with the
children and I forgot.'

—Sue Wall

So hold on to the ones who
really care. In the end they'll be
the ones who are still truly there.

—K. Hanson

Love life for better or worse,
without reservations.

—Arthur Rubinstein

Each day silently affirm that
you are the type of person with
whom you would want to spend
the rest of your life.

—Bob Moawad

125

When you've only one breath left,
use it to say thank you.

—Pam Brown

Believe in your dreams.

Believe in today.

Believe that you are loved.

Believe that you make a difference.

Believe we can build a better world.

Believe when others might not.

Believe there's light at the end of the tunnel.

Believe that you may be that light

for someone else.

Believe that the best is yet to be.

Believe in yourself.

I believe in you.

Kobi Yamada

I will
remember you.
Will you
remember me?
Don't let your life
pass you by.

—Sarah McLachlan

Also available from Compendium Publishing are these spirited and compelling companion books of great quotations.

Be Happy.
Remember to live, love, laugh and learn.

Because of You™
Celebrating the Difference You Make™

Brilliance™
Uncommon Voices From Uncommon Women™

Forever Remembered™
A Gift for the Grieving Heart.™

Little Miracles™
To renew your dreams, lift your spirits, and strengthen your resolve.™

Reach for the Stars™
Give up the Good to Go for the Great.™

Thank You™
In appreciation of you, and all that you do.™

Together We Can™
Celebrating the Power of a Team and a Dream.™

To Your Success™
Thoughts to Give Wings to Your Work and Your Dreams™

Whatever It Takes™
A Journey into the Heart of Human Achievement™

You've Got a Friend™
Thoughts to Celebrate the Joy of Friendship™

These books may be ordered directly from the publisher (800) 914-3327.
But please try your bookstore first!

www.compendiuminc.com